*Landing* starts on a plane and takes us to places around the world, from a lake in Maine to the streets of Tokyo, from an Irish church to the pyramids of Egypt. But despite this expansiveness, Kirkham anchors these poems in the smallest of details: a fish "silver and transfigured," the "yellow silk" of a globeflower, the crows who "clipped a clothing hanger to their nest." *Landing* is ultimately an emotional journey into the depths of memory, and the path is vibrant with color and nourished by ever-present waters. You're going to want to come along.
—**MATTHEW J. ANDREWS**, author of *The Hours*

Nora Kirkham crafts a poetic terrain that unassumingly cracks open the distance between body, self, earth, and the divine, only to reassemble them in a transfigured, animate frame. If you have ever felt a deep sense of homesickness—even for a place that doesn't exist—her poetry will bring you home.
—**GABRIELA MILKOVA ROBINS**, poet

# Landing

*Poems*

Nora Kirkham

Solum Literary Press
2205 W Broadway A-119
Anaheim, CA 92804

solumpress.com

PARERBACK ISBN 978-1-965169-02-5
EBOOK ISBN 978-1-965169-03-2

Cover art and design by Sarah Christolini.
Interior design by Riley Bounds.
Author photo by Nora Kirkham. Used with permission.

LIBRARY OF CONGRESS CATALOGUING-IN-PUBLICATION DATA
Name: Kirkham, Nora, author.
Title: Landing / nora kirkham.
Description: Anaheim, CA: Solum Literary Press, 2025.
Identifiers: LCCN 2024942692
ISBN: 978-1-965169-00-1 (print)
ISBN: 978-1-965169-03-2 (Kindle)
Subjects: BISAC: POETRY / Subjects & Themes / Places | Motivational & Inspirational | Women Authors
LC record available at https://lccn.loc.gov/2024942692

These are the poems of my early twenties.
They are dedicated to my grandparents, Wilna and Floyd (Bud) Hall, and Bruce and Kathy Kirkham, who taught me the language of tree houses, time capsules, fairy houses.

"In the beginning I was so young and such a stranger to myself that I barely existed. I had to go out into the world and see it and hear it and react to it, before I knew at all who I was, what I was, what I wanted to be."

Mary Oliver, *Upstream*

"Love is a landscape the long mountains define but don't shut off from the unseeable distance."

Denise Levertov, "Love Song"

# Contents

## Ruin Time

# Preface

*You must be in the air by now.* A text message shuffles onto my phone right before I lose connection. The plane lifts its steel-white body from the ground and rises. There is an ache in my ears that travels down to my heart, settling on my knees. There is a new wind pressing against a damp window and I turn to it, retracing a map of hidden places.

Somewhere there is a green lake and my mother is swimming in it. On a peninsula the size of a fingerprint, there is a forest of creaking trees, and my father is slicing away at the fallen pine. My sisters and I have scattered ourselves above and beneath the equator. We remember incense sticks smoking, cramped subways, bells ringing on mountains, our bodies burnt by the sun and healed by the sea. Somewhere even further, there is a glistening gold leaf panel of a Madonna, a spilled cup of tea, a field aflame with fireweed and gorse, a transfigured fish, and more moons.

These poems are reaching down into the roots of experience, bringing them beside each other and holding them as they have held me for years. To write is to return, resurrect, and prepare for landing.

# LANDING

# Globe Flower

## Afresh

A song was wound in my head
like wild grass under stone,
and memory clung like a spider
web spun in a mailbox.

The swamp I passed was
a city sunken in pools of fresh ink.
In its reflection
every ghostly limb grew whiter.

But this morning I saw the sea.
Heaven blue in an opposite way.
It was straight and unsolvable—
I held its gaze.

# Not the Ascent

I was growing with the mountain,
and rising to meet its breath.
I found my filled hips level with the glacier,
and lifted my eyes to it as I was taught to do,
blinding myself blue with the frosted sky.
I asked the mountain if it would hold me,
and before it could reply, I knew it was not
the ascent I wanted, but something else.
It was chasing the last glint of moon
on a fox tail, running off-trail
through a cloud of wet flowers,
and sinking into their cold honey
as each stem towered above my spine.
It was listening for that ongoing
clang of cowbells swelling in each bud,
until I no longer cursed the spiders
living below for bites that bled black.
It was remembering how I had passed
this field so many times and wondered
what would fly from its waving grass.
The stillness asked me where I was
and I did not know how to answer.
I had not been looking at all.
Now, I was growing again with the mountain,
falling to meet its breath through each tree
entering my lungs, until all I carried
was the wind and the wind was carrying me.
I asked the mountain again if it would hold
my body and bring me closer to itself,
to love me beyond all disbelief.
It was not the ascent it wanted from me,
but something else, and it was blooming.

# Damariscotta

We drive Downeast
leaving Atlantic salt
for a freshwater lake.

I enter the shallow end
with my legs close together
and cover my thighs
so they shrink
behind the shadow
of my hands.

My mother is waiting for me
among the loons and wild lilies,

calling to me from this lake
where she stood
twenty-eight years ago
and waded
as I rocked inside of her.

She draws me
through weeds and ripples
until I return
to her side, unfolding
my arms from my legs

so we are both
floating,
nestled by waves
that rise and fall between us.

# The Sun is Our Witness

My sisters and I are split
by the equator—

this band of light
hides us for half a decade
from snow and saltwater pools,
pine roads and frangipani juice.

We send letters north
and south, folding each page
down the middle

like a waxed leaf closing
over the stem, or the root—

our pens become bodies
leaking flowers and salt
for one another
as dark ink fades and sets
into long sheets of sun.

# Globe Flower

We traveled up this way in silence,
only mentioning the small strawberries,
cowslip and pine, and the low shining
bells in the valley below.

I thought I heard a bell inside a globeflower,
all yellow silk, enclosing a chime
within its curled petals as we climbed higher

before we turned from the snow and clouds,
scattering down a stinging hill of nettles.

I could have said more to you in the thunder
when we were mud and mountain and stranger.

You washed your face and hid the cloth
in your pocket, smudged with the summit.
It is still stained on the descent. This happened.
I will never know what it all meant.

# Meadow

Where the hot air is honeyed with weeds
and buds that burst yellow in dreams,
you are more golden in the morning.

Beetles and birds beat their wings,
flipping wind-paper backs in a frenzy.
Like a hive cracked open in harvest,
their work spills thick and runs below
unmoved snow in a mountain bowl.

And you wake, every moment,
weathered and blessed with a burn
from a light that never stops longing.

# Green Lake

My mind swims in my mother's lake,
a green lake, a deep lake, softer than mud.

Before she taught me how to swim,
my feet sunk into tangled carpets of weeds.

With our hands, we dug and drizzled
soaked sand into salted kingdoms.
I lowered silver minnows into their moats.

Our bodies were the lake, washed in green.
I saw my grandmother and grandfather live
and float towards its center, a glowing sun.

Then I drove myself under lily pads,
remembering anything we gave to the weeds—
a bathing suit, a ring, all washed in green.

There is a sign in my grandfather's house
that says "Love One Another."

I could never leave without looking at the lake.
How could we forget its power? Its glistening,
green waves return to us all that slips—

a minnow fin, a dream of floating and becoming
a lake where nothing bright is lost.

# At the Surface

*For Floyd Hall*

On the lake this morning,
we only listen and look—

we are still at the center.
Our lines are lowered, and we wait
for the pull of weight underwater,
a quick splash, or a turning glint.

You teach me to hold onto this
line with all my heart,
the line that connects our lives
to everything else under the surface.

Sometimes, the water tugs—
we reel flopping silver into our arms,
and fill our boat with the rest of life
where I will keep remembering you.

# Crossing

You might arrive before my train leaves
just to drop my bags behind my seat
when I leave alone for a new city.

I invent a story about these doors—
they could snap shut
before you have time to jump.

You're still here, leaning in the aisle,
welded to me like a track sparking
for a few more seconds.

I will pass through hours of pine
and glowing fireweeds without a witness
once these doors flash
and you alight the train,

once you reach that vast platform
with the whole world ringing, waving back.

# Access

We pull over at the field towards the church, slip
under wires, clamber over crackled walls.
You wade into a chamber of sun-soaked grass.

Centuries ago, the roof fell open to rain. Today
the clouds smudge sheep backs into shadows.
An archway awakens you to the coolness of being.

And walking in procession towards the cross, circling
sunken stones, I press sponge moss against my palms.
A hawthorn tree grows behind the wall, watching us glide

between fairy lines and we wander back to the car.
Its branches bend to marry the morning and night.
And we have learned to love the late winter light.

# Tidal Body

# Sea Baptism

Now every year if you return to this water,
find familiar driftwood in their place and
rock-weed necklaces dressing the shore.

Do you remember how the chilled sea
snapped as you entered the cove?

A common tern split the air and dove
through the waves and returned, a fish
thick in its beak, silver and transfigured.

Is it possible to hold this light again?

When the water splashes your neck,
dislodge the roots underfoot. Unhinge
the clam shell, say yes and sing.

# Tidal Body

She says there are tides in the body,
and time rises in the blood like a wave.

Before it breaks, I feel it crest inside of me,
colliding with each tired vessel as it leaves.

The wave rinses out a month of colors
until I exhale an empty shore,
and iron with red crusts on my knees.

I keep walking, dripping the moon, and pinch
the inside of my thigh so I won't drift away.

# The Buoy

*"There is a grey eye which ever turns to Erin."*
*—St. Columba (AD 521–597)*

I would have latched a message along its side
for the fishermen in Clare who found it
this morning, battered and crusted
with goose barnacles and saddleback oysters
riding along iced waves.

For weeks, this Maine buoy
swept across the dark Atlantic.
Unlatched from its pine-bright bay,
it dove under the wind with seals
until it reached a landing of spring gorse.

I would have slipped my hands underwater
had I been there to find it first,
to see if anything else had drifted this way.

Shadows would swim as I cup the cold sea,
the distance spilling out between my fingers,
knowing it had been here was enough.

# Village Church

*Doolin, County Clare*

Beneath the open pews,
I pause under a glass knot
in a window glistening
with Saint Patrick.

Someone once came to feast here,
taking the long road past
lamb meadows, arriving
just before the old hymns slowed.

I drop a coin to hear
an iron open-mouthed echo,
snap a light on a candle,
and bring it to the middle.

Among plaster hands and painted eyes,
a world within is still watching,

holding me and someone else
in the first flame of the morning.

# Faddan More Psalter

*National Museum of Ireland*

The leather book fell open on a slice of mud.
The digger found its peat shrine,
and his shovel clung to the Psalm:

*In the Valley of Tears, a place he has set,*
*The giver of the law shall give a blessing.*
*The autumn rain covers the land with water.*
*They go from strength to strength.*

The cows grazed like shades in the mist.
Their frames faded into the standing earth.
And their heads stayed low below the pines,
black mouths to green blades.

# North Sea

The sea sings on warm, white wings
and drifts into blue hills.

The clouds sink into spring
until gorse is soft and gold again:
coconut mist to dull the sharpest thistle.

## Yorkshire Tea

I made my tea like yours,
a full splash of milk so
it was lighter than I prefer
like a dried oak leaf.

And it was a little
by accident, that night
I spilled
boiling water down my leg.

My skin stung white.
I called you to hear you say that
all I needed was cold water.

Every kindness in the world
happened right there.

In the porcelain,
an amber sphere brightened
like a harvest moon
before the gathering light departed.

# Bright Wind

I recognized you when you spoke my name
in dawn's light patterned within window frames.

You brightened every pine bough in high summer,
and arrived again in moments—as if you were ever away—

returning with a fierceness that stung my jaw
when I opened my mouth to the sea and breathed.

And you spoke with a force that wills everything,
sweeping stiff clothes white, alive to living.

Your bright wind flickered as new branches grew.
Even when I am blind—*darkness is not dark to you.*

# On Folding

# Ginza Line

We thread ourselves through
this orange subway line,
stitching spine to spine.

We are closer to something else
than we will ever be,

or maybe just a gloss advertisement
of a woman, twisting open
a long, black bottle of mascara.

We all look at her, unstitching
ourselves from each other
when she blinks.

# A Red Dragonfly

The dragonfly was my mother tongue;
it perched, glittering in my mouth.

Every night, I walked home
to a going-home song,
and a rabbit danced inside a moon
as tadpoles spun into spring.

I sang about all of these things
before the dragonfly flew away.

The only word left is *akatombo*.
That red dragonfly catches me
like a flower bud blossoming
in the back of my throat.

If I knew the rest, could I return?
Could I string myself back together
like a line of lanterns to relight the sky?

## Before I Turned Around

While I was slicing tomatoes,
worried that you might
sneak in a heavy helping
of salt,
you quietly pressed
a Band-Aid
to my bleeding ankle.

## At the Onsen

At the old inn's bath,
my mother and I sit beside a mirror,
our sides swept in rising steam.

I wrap my arms around my chest
and all the parts she has not seen.

The moon is filled to its rim
with honey gold,
holding itself above the river
at Kanmangafuchi Abyss.

Tonight, the river pounds
above the sound of my mother
tipping a bowl of warm water
along her spine.

I follow her, tip-toed
into the tub with pools of soap
at my heels, slipping into

the scalding silence
that presses itself against a river
and rice paper walls.

# Matsu (松)

This word for pine sounds like waiting,
the way trees rise around a shrine, tied
with hemp ropes, their resin aching
for a god to descend.

In another country, my father
plants a pinecone under leaves,
marking its place on a plank in kanji.

This sign sinks into the soil
as the cone takes root and crosses
fungi threads on its descent
towards a bedrock of sparkling quartz.

This seedling is a prayer that drinks
from the rock and a word like waiting,
reaching out to winged voices
on higher branches,

until the tired and far-flung words spread
into a sharp green forest, pining
for something old and something else.

# Freeing the Fox

When the tepee collapsed,
a chickadee flew
through its birch skeleton.
Campfire stumps in soaked pine dew.
The woods were still the woods.

My father once hid among the trees
to build it with long branches,
clearing pinecones and spider curtains
from the ground.

On a skirt of white canvas,
he created a fox with a fresh snout
that nipped red paint on his thumbs,
and he might have hummed
as he dabbed black into its gleaming eyes.

He might have freed the fox
by cutting it from the canvas just before
a snowstorm overturned the tepee.

The fox trailed behind him to our cabin
where it would stay to tame our dreams
from a picture frame dry with mosquito wings.

My father and the fox guard all they see.
They outran years of rising snow before
that tepee fell to rotting bark.
On country roads, my father is always
breaking for foxes in the dark.

# On Folding

*Arisugawa Park, Tokyo*

I ride the subway all day, rising from the station
and descending into it with rain-like breathing.
For seventeen years, I have practiced folding
and unfolding, first with paper,
then with myself.
With each crease, I marked new miles
leaving familiar trees, bodies of water, and stars,
then returned on the sparking wheels of a plane,
folding myself back into the city where it started,
counting the years I was away.
The city unfolded itself with hidden lights,
opening like a snow crane as it lifts one fanned wing
while standing still in the mud.
I had been content to watch a crane fly
across winding rolls of paper, to live in scratches
of gold-flecked pine, descending
to a corner far away, to stay put and not return
to the place that left the deepest crease.
All day, the subway bends and tracks these lines.
I descend back into glistening tunnels before I rise.
Here is a small station behind a pond.
I think I saw something in the center of it,
sky-white and long-legged as it rained.
Here is my life laid out and open for walking again.

# Kathleen

She knits the sea
between us with white yarn,
stitching a circle
into a scarf to hug my neck.
She makes my winters warm.

In ten years, I will summon the scarf
from a drawer in another country,
restitching my skin to her sea.

Even as the first snow falls
and she drifts farther and farther,

each row will knit us back together
like pine branches sealed in sunlit ice.

I have seen this happen before
from her kitchen window:
trees leaning on each other,
waiting with silver limbs
for a white-stomached chickadee to land.

# Morning Crows

They clipped a clothing hanger to their nest
outside our home, white hooks stitched
between twigs and missing things.

They stole a bundle of soft toast in a
napkin thrown across our neighbor's roof.
Butter shimmered on their wings.

In a trance I watched them perched
on the edge of a branch, as they dropped
bread and worms into pink, loud mouths.

They flew where we could not follow,
clawing the sky between the city's towers.
I hear their caws echo in the early hours.

Before I rest my legs on the family bed,
I might open a window, hear them lifting
their dark bodies. I might lose them.

# Ruin Time

# Ruin Time

*"Time creates the ruin by making it something other
than what it was. Time writes the future of
a ruin."—Florence M. Hetzler*

The descent is not what you imagine.
Inside this desert, lotus blossoms float
along the halls of the Nile.
This pyramid holds the weight of it,
the golden reeds, the owls, the water.
The world around this tomb is warm
and the way here will require you to bend,
to make absence into something else.
Some loves die slow deaths, but not yours.
You have set it aside for an afterlife,
taking the words from within your ribs
and sealing them in jars of darkness.
They stay there, unmoved, even as
you return to them as someone different,
even as the painted stars on this ceiling
fade into new lights beneath the sand.

# Annunciation (Epilogue)

She returned to the abbey in Kilkenny this morning,
expecting to find everything in its place:

Stained glass spun like a sundial
to pierce her vision.
She returned to the carved, crossed legs.
How she clung to this station
and the sweet dampness that accompanied
every inhale.

She floated her fingers down her breast.
North, South, East, West—again, across her chest.
Daylight pooled between the pillars.

This was the way she reentered, with incense
on her heart, and the quick, forbidden thought—
Though He was listening, sometimes
it was all too strange.

# February Sky

The air is deep like a lake
when we walk uphill, breathing in winter's
cold water with the birds, and out
with the dark branches.

       Something will break through,
          the walk home will brighten.

The cloud ahead is a mountain
with wide gashes of light, breathing
into us before the night breaks.

       Tomorrow, we get to do this again.

# Anyway, Don't Be A Stranger

*After "Scott Street" by Phoebe Bridgers*

*We have won the cosmic lottery,*
you tell me over the phone.
I sit cross-legged on the beach,
poking circles in the first layer of sand.

*That we exist at all is a miracle.*
I make mandalas with my hands,
watch strangers in the waves,
and love them for the tattoos on their legs.

I won't tell you what I am seeing here,
but burrow one hand through the sand
until it cools into darker crystals.

I am secretly remembering
standing next to you before a mirror,
our elbows nearly knocking
as we brushed our teeth in time,
maybe even surprised this was happening.

I won't ask you to believe in anything,
even if I am afraid of the world forgetting
us in front of that bathroom sink.

There is more sand to sift as I listen to you
and the white-winged miracles that keep
calling to each other across the water.
Before this, all we did was talk.

# From the Grass

We are on the train home from Aberdeen:
the hills are beginning to spring. You trail gorse
along a smudged window and spot deer,
a whole family of them, folded in a field.
Unfolding before your eyes, you thought
they were hares or birds. I wondered
how many creatures we had passed, how many
lived and died by us without ever knowing
they were seen, and if this matters, anyway.
In June I was in Salisbury, on a bus cresting
up a hill. Beyond the cathedral, a gold-leaf
glow spilled from glass windows and
I saw antlers flying, or maybe I dreamed.
From that bus window, I held on
to three light seconds of hooves lifting,
to the twisting of clover roots and soil
spreading only a millimeter further than
where it had been before.
Perhaps none of this mattered,
but I did not want to arrive at the next stop,
I wanted to turn back, I did not want to go
home. Some might call this haunting, how
these hidden lives breathe their way
up through new strands of grass—
they pass through us all the time. Sometimes,
from a window, we find them,
then forgetting is what makes them fly.

# The Shroud of Turin

On Friday I ride into town on the 216,
taking a seat beside the old women and waiting mother.

I see your face printed on a poster, a glimpse
of your burial linen on a framed square behind the driver.

Your mouth drops in tones of yellow ochre.
Your eyelids are sealed iron doors.
A man leans his cheek against you, then turns away.

How dark is it in there?
How bright is this love you are casting into the chasm—
even as your own wrists pale and fall?

We are coming to a stop now.
Someday, maybe, you will tell me what the space
between you and me looked like,
if any of us will remember this at all.

# Moving the Mountain

*Zabbaleen City, Cairo*

Every scrap from our houses has made it here
in a mass of ripped bags under rusted crosses.

We hid them in other hands
within the cleft of a mountain cracked open.
We forget this trail of plastic thread
could catch flame at any moment.

This is where a saint carried waterskins
to the edge of the smoking city,
blinding himself in one eye
so he would not sin—he only needed one eye
to move this mountain, one mustard seed
in his palm to split it open.

He planted that seed in the wreckage
until it broke into yellow blossoms.
Its roots spread under the streets like an echo,
to cast what we hide into blinding gold.

# A Madonna in Orvieto

*After* Madonna Della Misericordia, *painted by*
*Lippo Memmi*

I was a peasant girl before heaven
threw the moon under my feet.

I shook off olive dust for a crown
and gathered myself in golden light

because I was told the womb is
the window to the crucified curse.

Your ancestors trembled within
the milk shelter of my cloak,

singing *despise not our petitions*,
swinging incense and praying,

bless our soil and our swords.
And how could they know that

I do not look at them as I stand,
but only at you and how many

hundreds of generations before
you did I lift up to the ceiling?

How many generations after
you will we unfold our hands

and meet in a holy gaze renewed,
still mortal, still together?

# Even if You Let Yourself Go Fallow

No one saw how the storm
brought that giant pine to the earth.

It fell on frozen ground and choked
chilled roots that had been waiting.

When summer swept the woods, blackberries
pushed their way through its peeling trunk.

My father sawed it apart, splitting rings,
and loading my arms with their weight.

Where there was a stump, there are trees.
We almost miss them until they spring back:
sharp, fresh hints from the soil.

## Acknowledgments

"Afresh" was originally featured in *Ruminate Magazine*.
"Not the Ascent" is in *Amethyst Review*.
"Access" was published in *St. Katherine Review*.
"Meadow" and "The Shroud of Turin" were published in *Ekstasis Magazine*.
"Morning Crows" was featured in *Tokyo Poetry Journal*.
"Bright Wind" was published in *The Christian Century*.
"From the Grass" was published in *Brain Mill Press*.
"Green Lake," "Yorkshire Tea," and "Damariscotta" were originally featured in *Macrina Magazine*.
"Sea Baptism" and "Annunciation (Epilogue)" were published in *Clayjar Review*.
"At the Onsen" was originally featured in *Peregrine*.
"Ruin Time" was published in *Red Noise Collective*.
"The Buoy" was published in *Paperbark Magazine*.
"Freeing the Fox" was featured in *Sheila-na-Gig*.
"On Folding" and "A Red Dragonfly" were featured in *Among Worlds Magazine*.
"A Madonna in Orvieto" (previously titled "Sub Tuum Praesidium") was published by *Orvieto Mostra* in Orvieto, Italy.
"Matsu (松)" was featured in *Arboreal Magazine*.

www.ingramcontent.com/pod-product-compliance
Lightning Source LLC
Chambersburg PA
CBHW030814090426
42737CB00010B/1268